Las Fuerzas Armadas de EE.UU./
The U.S. Armed Forces

Los Thunderbirds de la Fuerza Aérea de EE.UU./

The U.S. Air Force Thunderbirds

por/by Carrie A. Braulick

Consultora/Consultant:
Barbara J. Fox
Especialista en Lectura/Reading Specialist
Universidad del Estado de Carolina del Norte/
North Carolina State University

Mankato, Minnesota

Blazers is published by Capstone Press,
151 Good Counsel Drive, P.O. Box 669, Mankato, Minnesota 56002.
www.capstonepress.com

Copyright © 2007 by Capstone Press. All rights reserved.
No part of this publication may be reproduced in whole or in part, or stored in a retrieval system, or transmitted in any form or by any means, electronic, mechanical, photocopying, recording, or otherwise, without written permission of the publisher. For information regarding permission, write to Capstone Press,
151 Good Counsel Drive, P.O. Box 669, Dept. R, Mankato, Minnesota 56002.
Printed in the United States of America

Library of Congress Cataloging-in-Publication Data
Braulick, Carrie A., 1975–
   [Thunderbirds. Spanish & English.]
   Los Thunderbirds de la Fuerza Aérea de EE.UU./por Carrie A. Braulick = The U.S. Air Force Thunderbirds/by Carrie A. Braulick.
   p. cm.—(Blazers—Las Fuerzas Armadas de EE.UU. = Blazers—The U.S. Armed Forces)
   Includes index.
   ISBN-13: 978-0-7368-7750-3 (hardcover)
   ISBN-10: 0-7368-7750-9 (hardcover)
   1. United States. Air Force. Thunderbirds—Juvenile literature. 2. Stunt flying—Juvenile literature. I. Title. II. Title: U.S. Air Force Thunderbirds.
UG633.B72518 2007
797.5'40973—dc22   2006027474

Summary: Describes the U.S. Air Force Thunderbirds, including their planes, the maneuvers at their air shows, and team member duties—in both English and Spanish.

Credits
Juliette Peters, set designer; Patrick D. Dentinger, book designer; Jo Miller, photo researcher; Scott Thoms, photo editor; Strictly Spanish, translation services; Saferock USA, LLC, production services

Photo Credits
Art Directors/Maxwell Mackenzie, 25
Corbis/George Hall, 17; William Manning, 22–23
DVIC/SRA Greg L. Davis USAF, 12, 19
George Hall/Check Six, 14 (bottom), 26
Getty Images Inc./AFP/Kim Jae-Hwan, 6, 7
Photo by Ted Carlson/Fotodynamics, 13, 14 (top), 28–29
Photri-Microstock, cover, 11
USAF Air Demonstration Squadron, Media Relations, cover (inset); SSgt. Sean White, 5, 8, 19 (inset), 20–21, 27
Zuma/Art Seitz, 18

Capstone Press thanks MSgt. George F. Jozens, public affairs superintendent, U.S.A.F. Thunderbirds, for his assistance in preparing this book.

1 2 3 4 5 6 12 11 10 09 08 07

Table of Contents

The Thunderbirds in Action 4
Thunderbird Planes 10
Maneuvers 16
Thunderbird Jobs 24

Delta Positions 22
Glossary 30
Internet Sites 30
Index 32

Tabla de contenidos

Los Thunderbirds en acción 4
Aviones de los Thunderbirds 10
Maniobras 16
Empleos de los Thunderbirds 24

Posiciones delta 22
Glosario 31
Sitios de Internet 31
Índice 32

The Thunderbirds in Action

The Thunderbird planes glide into the air. People in a large crowd are excited for the show to begin.

Los Thunderbirds en acción

Los aviones de los Thunderbirds se deslizan por los aires. Un numeroso público se emociona con el inicio del espectáculo.

Four planes fly beside each other in the diamond formation. They make a large loop.

Cuatro aviones vuelan lado a lado en la formación diamante. Hacen un rizo grande.

Opposing knife-edge pass/
Cruce filo de cuchillo

The pilots continue showing off their exciting moves. Later, the show ends. People in the crowd rush to meet the pilots.

Los pilotos siguen mostrando sus emocionantes movimientos. El espectáculo termina un poco después. El público se acerca a conocer a los pilotos.

Blazer Fact

In American Indian legends, Thunderbirds were large creatures that made the earth shake when they flew.

Dato Blazer

En las leyendas de los indios nativos americanos, los *thunderbirds* (pájaros de trueno) eran criaturas grandes que hacían temblar la tierra cuando volaban.

Thunderbird Planes

The U.S. Air Force Thunderbirds perform daring moves with planes. Their first planes were Thunderjets.

Aviones de los Thunderbirds

Los Thunderbirds de la Fuerza Aérea de EE.UU. realizan osadas maniobras con los aviones. Sus primeros aviones se llamaban Thunderjets.

Thunderjets/Thunderjets

Today, Thunderbirds fly F-16 Fighting Falcons. These fighter jets are fast and easy for pilots to control.

Actualmente, los Thunderbirds vuelan aviones F-16 Fighting Falcon. Estos jets de combate son rápidos y los pilotos los pueden controlar fácilmente.

Blazer Fact

Many pilots call F-16s "Vipers." As F-16s land, some people think they look like pit viper snakes.

Dato Blazer

Muchos pilotos llaman "Vipers" (víboras) a los F-16. Algunas personas piensan que al aterrizar los F-16 parecen víboras.

Control stick/Palanca de control

Pilots use cockpit equipment to fly the planes. They use a control stick to change directions.

Los pilotos usan equipo de cabina para volar los aviones. Usan una palanca de control para cambiar de dirección.

Maneuvers

High-speed maneuvers are the heart of a Thunderbird show. Rolls, loops, and dives thrill crowds.

Maniobras

Las maniobras a alta velocidad son el corazón de un espectáculo de los Thunderbirds. Toneles, rizos y caídas emocionan al público.

Bomb burst/Estallido de bomba

17

Many maneuvers include formations. The delta formation is shaped like a triangle. Four planes make an arrowhead formation in the arrowhead loop.

Muchas maniobras incluyen formaciones. La formación delta tiene forma de triángulo. En el rizo punta de flecha, cuatro aviones hacen una formación de punta de flecha.

Blazer Fact

The Thunderbirds' delta formation is named after the fourth letter of the Greek alphabet.

Dato Blazer

La formación delta de los Thunderbirds toma su nombre de la cuarta letra del alfabeto griego.

Delta/Delta

Arrowhead/
Punta de flecha

Crossover break/Pase cruzado

Sometimes, one or two planes are the center of attention. In the crossover break, two planes cross paths.

A veces uno o dos aviones son el centro de atención. En el pase cruzado, dos aviones se cruzan en el camino.

Delta Positions/Posiciones delta

- Commander/Comandante
- Left wing/Ala izquierda
- Right wing/Ala derecha
- Lead solo/Solista líder

Thunderbird Jobs

The pilots in shows are not the only Thunderbirds. Other team members fix planes, plan shows, and do other jobs.

Empleos de los Thunderbirds

Los pilotos de los espectáculos no son los únicos miembros de los Thunderbirds. Otros miembros del equipo arreglan aviones, planean espectáculos y realizan otros trabajos.

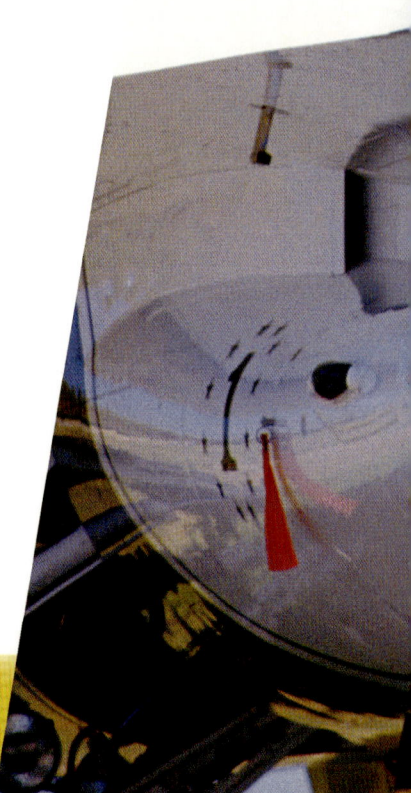

All Thunderbirds train for their jobs. New pilots learn each maneuver before they fly in shows. Skilled pilots keep shows both exciting and safe.

Todos los Thunderbirds se entrenan para su trabajo. Los nuevos pilotos aprenden cada maniobra antes de volar en espectáculos. Los pilotos experimentados hacen que los espectáculos sean emocionantes y seguros a la vez.

Bon-ton roulle/Tonel elegante

Flying in the diamond formation/Vuelo en la formación diamante

Glossary

cockpit—the area in the front of a plane where the pilot sits

control stick—the lever in a plane's cockpit that a pilot uses to steer

delta—the six-plane formation of the Thunderbirds

diamond—a formation in which four Thunderbird planes form a diamond shape

fighter jet—a fast plane designed to destroy enemy aircraft

formation—a group of planes flying together in a pattern

maneuver—a planned and controlled movement

roll—to turn sideways in a complete circle

Internet Sites

FactHound offers a safe, fun way to find Internet sites related to this book. All of the sites on FactHound have been researched by our staff.

Here's how:
1. Visit *www.facthound.com*
2. Choose your grade level.
3. Type in this book ID **0736877509** for age-appropriate sites. You may also browse subjects by clicking on letters, or by clicking on pictures and words.
4. Click on the **Fetch It** button.

FactHound will fetch the best sites for you!

Glosario

el avión de combate—un avión rápido diseñado para destruir aeronaves enemigas

la cabina—el área al frente del avión donde se sienta el piloto

delta—la formación de seis aviones de los Thunderbirds

el diamante—una formación en la que cuatro aviones de los Thunderbirds forman un diamante

la formación—un grupo de aviones que vuelan juntos en un patrón

la maniobra—un movimiento planeado y controlado

la palanca de control—la palanca en la cabina que el piloto utiliza para dirigir el avión

el tonel—girar lateralmente en un círculo completo

Sitios de Internet

FactHound proporciona una manera divertida y segura de encontrar sitios de Internet relacionados con este libro. Nuestro personal ha investigado todos los sitios de FactHound. Es posible que los sitios no estén en español.

Se hace así:
1. Visita *www.facthound.com*
2. Elige tu grado escolar.
3. Introduce este código especial **0736877509** para ver sitios apropiados según tu edad, o usa una palabra relacionada con este libro para hacer una búsqueda general.
4. Haz clic en el botón **Fetch It**.

¡FactHound buscará los mejores sitios para ti!

Index

cockpit, 15
control stick, 15
crowds, 4, 9, 16

F-16 Fighting Falcons, 12, 13
formations, 7, 18
　arrowhead, 18
　delta, 18
　diamond, 7

jobs, 24, 26

loops, 7, 16, 18

maneuvers, 7, 16, 18, 20, 26
　arrowhead loop, 18
　crossover break, 20

pilots, 9, 12, 13, 15, 24, 26

rolls, 16

Thunderjets, 10
training, 26

Índice

cabina, 15

entrenamiento, 26

F-16 Fighting Falcons, 12, 13
formaciones, 7, 18
　delta, 18
　diamante, 7
　punta de flecha, 18

maniobras, 7, 16, 18, 20, 26
　pase cruzado, 21
　rizo punta de flecha, 18

palanca de control, 15
pilotos, 9, 12, 13, 15, 24, 26
público, 4, 9, 16

rizos, 7, 16, 18

Thunderjets, 10
toneles, 16
trabajos, 24, 26